Chips

Story written by Gill Munton
Illustrated by Tim Archbold

Speed Sounds

Consonants

Ask children to say the sounds.

f	l	m	n	r	s	v	z	sh	th	ng
ff	ll					(ve)	s			nk

b	c	d	g	h	j	p	qu	t	w	x	y	(ch)
	k								wh			tch
	ck											

Each box contains one sound but sometimes more than one grapheme.
*Focus graphemes for this story are **circled**.*

Vowels

Ask children to say the sounds in and out of order.

a	e	i	o	u
at	hen	in	on	up

ay	ee	igh	ow	oo
day	see	high	blow	zoo

Story Green Words

Ask children to read the words first in Fred Talk and then say the word.

Kim   Sam   Jen   Tim

Ask children to read the root first and then the whole word with the suffix.

chip → chips

Red Words

Ask children to practise reading the words across the rows, down the columns and in and out of order clearly and quickly.

I	said	of
no	you	be
the	he	your
my	put	said

Chips

Kim had a big bag of chips.

"Can I have a chip?" said Sam.

"Yes," said Kim.

But Sam got *lots* of chips!

"Can I have a chip?" said Jen.

"Yes," said Kim.

But Jen got
lots of chips!

"Can I have a chip?" said Tim.

"Yes," said Kim.

But Tim got
lots of chips!

Kim had a big bag ...

but no chips!

Questions to talk about

Ask children to TTYP for each question using 'Fastest finger' (FF) or 'Have a think' (HaT).

p.9 (FF) How many chips did Sam ask for?

p.11 (FF) How many chips did Tim ask for?

p.13 (HaT) How did Kim feel when all her chips had gone?